About the author:

Linette Tyler was born in Chicago, Illinois.
As an infant, until the age of about nine years
old, Linette was raised on a plantation called
Belle Chase, in Mississippi, by her
grandparents along with their own children.
At about the age of nine, Linette and her
family were finally able to relocate from
Belle Chase Plantation and settled in
Greenwood, Mississippi, where she stayed
until the death of her grandmother. After the
death of her grandmother, Linette had to
move to Chicago in 1983, with her biological
mother and stepfather. Being away from her
grandfather, family, and friends, caused
Linette to deal with many emotional issues
that were difficult to handle and express to
others. She had to get used to being in a big
city with both a mother and stepfather she did
not know, while grieving in secret the death
of her grandmother and the separation of her
grandfather who she considered as her
parents. Linette credits her family struggle of
living on a plantation during her childhood
and life experiences living in Chicago during
her teen years to the present day, for her

creative writing inspiration, as it has been therapeutic for her along the way. Linette is on a life awakening journey and has invited you, the reader a long side through reading her inner thoughts and seeing the world through her "I".

How did I come up with writing quotes? One day I reflected on my life, from childhood to the present. My upbringing in the south, death of love ones, failed relationships, abandonment, health issues, financial disasters, emotional abuse, addiction, and my survival of it all, inspired me to write. I realized I had a lot to share that might help others and what better way to share than my own personal quotes in book form! I hope that at least one or more of my quotes will be beneficial to one who takes the time to read them all or just one. I hope it is therapeutic for you, just as it was for me. My quotes are not only from my personal experiences, but of observations of others I've had the pleasure to meet as well.

Note:

My quotes are not to disrespect or degrade any person or group. The pronouns/nouns used are not directed to anyone personally.
I am humbled that you are giving of your time to read my book and I thank you. I believe in helping others through positive thoughts, communication, efforts of sharing ideas, encouragement, and information.

*** There's no special order to my quotes, so buckle down because your mind will probably be all over the place, which is a good thing. I want readers to think about what each quote could possibly be in reference to and discuss it with others.

Acknowledgments:

I dedicate this book, to my two beautiful daughters: Briana, my favorite oldest, and Brittney, my favorite youngest. The two of them have taught me how giving love and support to others, helps me as well. I am honored and thankful to them both for their roles and support in my life. They are truly amazing! I am thankful to my mother Beth, who risked her life by birthing me and for being such an amazing grandmother. I'm also thankful to my father Willie C, for the wisdom he shared with me about life before his passing. I thank and acknowledge my stepfather Ron and my stepmother Mary, for being there for me.
* I'm most grateful for Dad and Ma, (maternal grandparents) Frank and Mary, who raised me as their own child until death broke us apart. The two of them were true examples of sacrificing for the sake of love and survivor. Life without them has been a true reminder to always appreciate the simple things and not so simple things in life.

To my supporters:

Love wholeheartedly those who you deem worthy of such love. Do not become disappointed if the same love you give is not returned. We are all different beings...Love is love, whether given or received, different or the same. The purpose and joy of it all is to have self-love and to give love to others as well.
I Love you and thank you,
I AM! ~ Linette Tyler

And Eye Quote

By: Linette Tyler

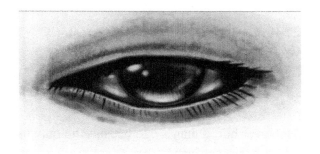

1.) Never allow yourself to hate another because hate is poisonous and destroys love.

2.) If one does not believe in his creator's works, how can he then be a believer in himself or you?

3.) Never hurt a man's ego because he may in return hurt your heart.

4.) If a person can't get over the mistakes of your past, take it as a warning that they might spoil happiness in your future.

5.) A child without a parent's presence in his life, could in the future be the equivalent of an elderly parent without his child's present in the time of need.

6.) I would rather break bread with an enemy than a trusted friend with a revengeful spirit whom I might have offended.

7.) In the workplace are many characteristics, the worse of all is jealousy.

8.) A friend will tell you the truth about a matter, if he does not then he is not your friend, you are his.

9.) One who spreads gossip about you is the one who can damage your image with lies among the ones who trust him.

10.) A gambler takes chances. It is therefore my theory, that everyone is a gambler.

11.) To love anyone unconditionally has a limit, called selflove.

12.) If it seems as everyone abandons you in relationships, then it's time to check yourself to see if you're all there.

13.) In your lifetime you have been a fool and you have been wise...What are you in your present situation?

14.) Walking away for the sake of love is better than crossing the line of hate.

15.) A person who talks a lot about everyone else has told you all you need to know about himself and about you who continues to listen.

16.) Double-minded could one day be double trouble.

17.) A rich friend loaning to a poor friend has ended the friendship and becomes a business partner.

18.) Being wise or having knowledge; of the two, wisdom is a great choice.

19.) It is ashamed to have read many books and not have made any wise decisions.

20.) One needing the validation of others is one who's not happy with oneself.

21.) A woman with a leader will follow him until he fails to give her direction.

22.) A spiritual person speaking evil is an evil spirit.

23.) Experience with no direction is self learning.

24.) Awaken each day with the expectations that something great and new will happen; It already has, you're alive.

25.) Running away from issues is the same as running into problems.

26.) Going on vacation to leave your problems behind is a wasted trip, unless one knows how to leave his own body.

27.) Never think too highly of yourself, it is then you are at your lowest level.

28.) A good leader listens to what appears to be the dumbest statement ever heard. That dumbest statement could be the smartest statement ever, if one hears what is being said.

29.) One who use lies, games, and deceit to gain love is one who loses love through lies, games, and deceit.

30.) All the therapy in the world won't save you from what's hidden in your heart, mind, and soul, if you never speak of the issues.

31.) Experience is the best way to learn. Without experience, one really doesn't know much at all.

32.) Loving them is easy. It's learning to like them that's difficult, when love happens at first sight.

33.) I love you dearly, yet I dislike you just as much. It is because of love I stay. It is because of love I must leave.

34.) Show me a person that constantly speaks to an audience and I'll show you a person who's constantly not listening!

35.) Be thankful for the beauty of darkness because light shows up better than ever at such a time.

36.) Being fearful of death could mean one is not enjoying life.

37.) How can One Love another when one doesn't know how to love himself or has ever been loved before?

38.) If the one you love doesn't love you back, change who you love. You will then realize you never truly loved them at all.

39.) Time can't be given back, yet in time, things come back to you.

40.) Parents and children teach one another discipline, love, and compassion. That's a family.

41.) Never say "as a matter of fact " if the fact isn't important to you.

42.) I love you, I like you, and I need you, are three phrases if spoken to you will make you want to stay in your mate's life and if spoken to them will make them want to stay in yours.

43.) Love me with a flawed past and I will love you with all your flaws now. Just love me as I am.

44.) The heart has got to be a strong muscle, because mine has been broken many times and I am still able to pick myself up and love again.

45.) Don't leave when times are hard, it's not a good idea. Leave when all is well, and your conscience will be clear.

46.) To lie and deceive in order to gain love is the heart of one who is afraid to be alone.

47.) A broken heart is one that trusted but was deceived and finds it difficult to trust again.

48.) Cancer can invade the body, mind, and spirit, but it cannot touch the soul of one who knows his purpose for living.

49.) An unforgiving heart is that of a person who has truly been hurt and gave up his power to the offender.

50.) One with knowledge is truly intelligent until he lacks understanding that wisdom is as good as knowledge.

51.) To be a user takes a lot of your time and effort. Who is using "you", the user?

52.) There's nothing wrong with helping others, when one remembers to one help himself as well.

53.) Never tell children to "shut up" when they are responding to your question or statement regarding their behavior. It lets them know that you too need discipline.

54.) One may not be the most intelligent person you've ever met, but one is able to teach you by wisdom and experience.

55.) To say to another, "I don't need your wisdom " is the dumbest statement one can ever make when claiming to be knowledgeable.

56.) Why be upset with a person that keeps disappointing you, they are not your upset. You are.

57.) Never play mind games with a person unless you don't mind Karma.

58.) A bully, when challenged, could become a coward; a coward could then become the bully. Neither are worth being fearful of.

59.) There's a difference in character and a character. Does one really know who he is or how to be himself?

60.) One can do a lot of good in the world just as much as one can do bad. Either way, one fits in.

61.) Belittling a person is an example of how small one feels about himself subconsciously.

62.) Uplifting someone when you yourself are dealing with issues, shows that there is greatness in you.

63.) Talking to yourself and answering yourself is not a problem, especially when you have no one else to trust other than yourself at that given moment.

64.) When speaking about purpose in life why not include the purpose of life, there is certainly a difference.

65.) I will follow your lead, if your lead is heading in the right direction.

66.) Compliments are appreciated but truth is usually rejected.

67.) To be separated from a spouse and struggle is a sure sign that you are single. Divorce is an option and so is reconciliation.

68.) I believe in miracles and I believe in blessings. I believe in me, because I am a miracle and I am blessed.

69.) There is no such thing as starting over in a relationship when things go wrong. There is such a thing as forgiving and moving forward or simply ending it.

70.) Estimating the power of love helps one to decide whether to walk away for the sake of love or stay because of love.

71.) If you can't disconnect from your past, try to focus more on connecting with the present. Chances are, you will have a better connection for the future.

72.) It is possible to love you and not like you, therefore it is possible to love you and leave you.

73.) To frown upon the way I live, is just as insulting as if I would frown upon the way you choose not to live.

74.) Some folk can't handle being corrected.
It is they who display wrong thought process.

75.) The hurt you feel is the hurt I feel as
well, because the love I have for you is as
deep as the love you have for yourself.

76.) I'm not myself if I give you all of me.

77.) Being too old for this and to young for
that; one somehow becomes balanced.

78.) Show me a man that loves his wife and
I'll show you a man who loves himself.

79.) Loyalty is so scarce in relationships that
to have such a thing is unbelievable.

80.) When your heart speaks my heart listens.
So far nothing is happening.

81.) I don't mind you controlling the situation, but I am strongly against mind control.

82.) Show me a person of complete submission to another and I'll show you one with an admission of being unhappy.

83.) Lust will cause a fool to stray from home and the power of love will cause him to return.

84.) In relationships, one might change his mind about the future, but be watchful of one who changes his heart concerning you.

85.) Encourage the children while they're young and they won't grow up seeking validation from others.

86.) One who socializes to the world through social media while in your company is one that lacks social skills and respect.

87.) One with a big ego and confidence can become a fool in a matter of seconds when offended in a conversation.

88.) If one fears being alone, one is fearful of oneself.

89.) Working to survive is normal. It is he who survives to work that's bothersome.

90.) Relationships last when respectable ones involved, agree to stay respectable and involved.

91.) My definition of a nonbeliever is one who does not believe in oneself.

92.) Money is known as the root of all evil. I think Sex is equal to money in relationships.

93.) Things easily gained are not appreciated as equally to things fought for and lost.

94.) Your life is different from others in many ways. It can be proven easily by looking in the mirror.

95.) No one is perfect unless he's in denial of ever having made a mistake. He then becomes a liar.

96.) Happiness is a feeling everyone has or will at some point experience. Saddness is the feeling of having lost the experience of happiness.

97.) Time is never wasted. It takes time to do absolutely nothing and more time to do everything.

98.) Never wish for your children to be as you are, wish them to be better than you could ever be.

99.) Be thankful that you have lived at such a time as this, otherwise you wouldn't exist.

100.) If you allow someone to treat you the same as they have treated others you are not special to them, they are special to you...

101.) Forgiveness is most definitely a task that if not conquered can probably cause Mental Abuse to oneself and then others...

102.) I call it "love limits" when one dislike you enough to leave you and doesn't seem to love you enough to stay.

103.) It is best to know that it's love than to think that it's love.

104.) A man and his woman are two. A man with his woman is one.

105.) Never be responsible for how a person feels about being in your presence. It is they who choose to allow you in or out of theirs.

106.) There's a difference in being single and being alone…Some married people are alone.

107.) Time alone is far greater than time spent in the company of one who doesn't value you.

108.) Never compare love. It's not a math issue, it's a heart issue without a formula.

109.) Keeping a secret can destroy you just as much as telling a secret can destroy others.

110.) One must realize that a mistake corrected still has consequences just as if not corrected at all.

111.) In order to love, one must have respect. In order to respect, one must trust. In order to trust, one must know "the one". I AM LOVE.

112.) Far away or close and near, time spent or no time at all, the love never ends if it's true love.

113.) Don't settle with being the doormat when you can just as easily be the carpet that the doormat protects.

114.) Many relationships fail because of assumptions. I assume it is safe to say that many lacks trust.

115.) The way to help one who has everything is to convince him to give up something. It teaches humbleness and that my friend, is very helpful.

116.) Each day is a new beginning. If one does the exact same as they did on yesterday, the day changes and the person remains the same.

117) Critical thinking is so important that if not done in a time of need could be critical.

118.) Chances are, the reasons why everything is failing is because something better hasn't been done.

119.) There are no dumb questions or statements if one thinks to ask and another speaks to answer.

120.) Minds are like time machines. One can travel the world, the past, and the future while being in the present moment, never moving. It's time to think...

121.) The best advice One can give is: You must believe that some things really are impossible. It is truly impossible to be anyone other than yourself.

122.) If one has the tit for tat attitude, why are you surprised by his actions? Did he not do what you have done in the first place?

123.) My biggest fear was to be alone until I found myself alone. I then realized that the fear I had was inner peace screaming for my attention...

124.) The person that loves you when you're away is probably the person that will never leave you when things go wrong.

125.) How can You follow your heart when your heart belongs to the one you love and they're not leading?

126.) Oddly as it may be, most are looking upon others on the outside to find what's sparkling on the inside of them.

127.) Changing because of someone's actions is not the same as changing for them. Always be yourself.

128.) Of all the things to feel or say about another, regret should not be on the list. Everyone is important.

129.) To save someone's life is a blessing, unless repayment is expected. It's then the killer of one spirit that needs to be saved.

130.) If love and compassion are for companions, how is it that one mistreats who loves him, yet gives compassion to another who is a stranger?

131.) Confused is the person who wants it all. Greed is his destruction and selfishness his weakness.

132.) There is nothing more disappointing than meeting that perfect one you dreamed of marrying, only to find they're in others dreams as well.

133.) Controlling people seems to be the ones that really lack self-control.

134.) To never sacrifice a thing for another is proof enough, they aren't as important as you make them to be.

135.) To push love away is that of a heart filled with fear, hurt, or hate.

136.) I would rather walk away for love than to stay in hostility, in love.

137.) The best way to never lose against a competitor person is to never compete.

138.) Time is too valuable to be in the presence of one who seeks to devalue you.

139.) A crazy person doesn't need a reason for his actions. He's crazy!

140.) Shame on the one who degrade others, does he not realize he's less than another based on his actions.

141.) The mind is strong enough to lift a person without ever lifting a finger. Pick yourself up.

142.) Give attention to what is important to you, if you don't, you'll surely give it away.

143.) The best type of man to marry is the man who appreciates why a woman was made.

144.) Never play games with a woman's heart when she truly loves you unless you are willing to have her tap out and walk away.

145.) I would rather be wealthy than rich with the possibility of being poor.

146.) Some marry and divorce their best-friend. Some later realize that they married and divorced a stranger instead.

147.) When the heart is burdened, it seeks to find happiness. Find happiness in knowing that your heart beats and you are alive.

148.) Writing and reading are good for the soul. A soul is happy right now.

149.) Life is good when one lives with goodness in his heart.

150.) Power is not the ability to control others, it's the ability to control oneself at difficult times.

151.) Why try to prove someone is a fool when you already know that they are? What a fool you yourself becomes.

152.) A wise woman in the company of a man with knowledge could be a threat to his ego and a boost to hers if he lacks wisdom.

153.) A person with many partners is probably one of the loneliest persons you'll ever meet.

154.) Speaking kind words is like medicine to the spirit, just as not speaking at all when you're angry.

155.) Child support seems to be more of a focus about giving money than it is about giving love and direction to the child.

156.) Don't confuse treating your mate proper with treating them as property. No person has the right to own another except for the creator of all.

157.) Never give everything to a person who feels privileged. Chances are, your giving is taken for granted and not appreciated.

158.) Children play games. An adult who deems himself as a player is probably not mentally able to handle adulthood.

159.) Never be afraid to walk away from abuse unless you are afraid of peace.

160.) An evil person thinks the worse of everything except for his own actions of causing misery to others.

161.) To speak publicly and not be able to handle criticism is one who probably should keep quiet.

162.) It is amazing how one person can change the mindset and actions of others, yet is too stubborn to change his own ways when he himself is wrong.

163.) Keep in mind that everyone is different. You shouldn't mind being the odd person in the room.

164.) A date can be perfect until one tries to prove being better than the other in some type of way.

165.) Be weary of one who attempts to prove love with flattery words or catering to your every need. Be also weary of one who demands such a thing be done. Love is a feeling that actions can't prove.

166.) Show me someone who needs validation and I will show you an insecure person who has been neglected in the past.

167.) To see greatness in one who sees no beauty in you is not foolish at all. It is greatness in you that knows everyone is different.

168.) Be sure that it is Love that makes you stay in a relationship and not the love of competition against another in the same position.

169.) A friend never tells a secret that will damage your reputation, but one who pretends to be your friend certainly will.

170.) The one who degrades you is probably one who fears your strength.

171.) Welcome to the world where everything matters, and nothing really matters at all. Welcome to life on earth.

172.) Be open to a new direction, it will take you to a place you've never been.

173.) If all love was the same, no one would need to love anyone if there's selflove.

174.) A deceitful mind is of one whom is living a lie and is a stranger to himself.

175.) Childhood memories and experiences are the result of the society we live in now. We all have issues.

176.) Being impossible to deal with is one who makes himself that way and blame others. He is possibly afraid of commitment.

177.) I find it best to have a friend to tell me when I'm wrong than to pretend that I am right. That is a faithful friend to have.

178.) You are just as valuable as the person who treats you as if you're no value at all.

179.) It's quite difficult to commit to someone who does not believe in being committed. Let it be understood that you're free.

180.) If you find yourself building someone and they are constantly tearing you down, you have got to find yourself.

181.) Speak with volume whether softly or aloud, just speak truthfully.

182.) If I could read minds, I would rather be alone.

183.) Don't want them to change who they are for you. Want them to change how they treat you because of who you are to them.

184.) Don't hesitate to do what makes you better unless it's morally wrong to do so.

185.) Never borrow from someone you respect as a friend. Friends don't loan to a friend and friends shouldn't have to borrow from a friend.

186.) To be angry at others about a situation you got yourself into is a lack of understanding of your responsibility or a lack of respect for others.

187.) Fantasies are better left alone, because once fulfilled, there's nothing more to look forward to.

188.) Surround yourself with people who set goals and are willing to help you do so if needed.

189.) At some point a person must realize that he's only as powerful as he believes himself to be.

190.) Fear of someone is different than the fear of something, unless someone is considered a monster.

191.) An apology without sincerity is that of a lying tongue that should not be trusted.

192.) Life has a way of happening everyday, even when we die.

193.) I never believed in stalkers until I met a person who refused to let go of a relationship that doesn't even exist.

194.) Love them for who they are and not for what they do. They can't stop being them, but they can stop doing what they do.

195.) Looks aren't everything because the heart is blind to love.

196.) A person competing for your love is the one you best not choose, because it's not you they love. It's the love of the game.

197.) A player using time playing many relationship games has no time to notice the person who is playing the player.

198.) I would rather walk away <u>for</u> the one I love, than walk away <u>from</u> the one I love. Love knows the difference.

199.) To gain love through deceit and manipulating of another's mind is the actions of a person with low self esteem meeting another with the same issue.

200.) It is best to be yourself and happy than to be miserable trying to be as others want you to be.

201.) Love is within and Love is without prejudice...Don't just feel it, know it. Life is about love.

202.) In order to make a statement, one sometimes need to make an exit.

203.) Most time the answer to a question asked is usually answered by the one asking the question.

204.) I would rather have experienced the pain of love than no love at all.

205.) When I look in the mirror, I see love and It's a beautiful site, because love is me...I AM love...

206.) I have known my place and my purpose. I know I'm important, otherwise, I would not exist.

207.) Oh, how one forgets to appreciate memories until the day one is unable to remember a simple thing.

208.) I've spoken many words to express myself. The best results I received, was when I said nothing at all.

209.) There's no sorrowful person than the one who does not forgive.

210.) To purposely avoid love is to purposely harm oneself.

211.) A woman gives her all to a man she loves without wanting anything in return.

212.) Foolish is the man who punish a woman who loves him by being absent. He only punishes himself with guilt when he's alone.

213.) Depression and happiness can be the result of relationships beginning or ending.

214.) The worse heartbreaks and disappointments are from loving a person who has no idea what love really is.

215.) Love is not supposed to be difficult. Love is peace when given and accepted.

216.) Sex is physical. Never confuse sex as an emotion of love.

217.) One who never apologize is one who could make others feel sorrowful.

218.) My love is deeper than my hurt, therefore, I suffer and stay because of love.

219.) There's no such thing as loving from afar. Love lives within.

220.) Rejection seems to keep a person trying, until one day the person rejects the rejection.

221.) If one bases a relationship from past issues, one will never have experience anything new.

222.) Some people <u>prey</u> on relationships and some <u>pray</u> on relationships.

223.) Never seek revenge against anyone who loves you. Seek peace instead.

224.) Never make your move hoping to make someone else move too. You might be making a wrong move

225.) If happiness is a choice, why are so many people unhappy?

226.) Wake up and accept that beauty was in your bed all night. You are beautiful!

227.) A prayer can be many words or just one word. Be humble and expect an answer.

228.) It's amazing how much energy is wasted to push love away. It's amazing how much energy is gained when love is accepted. The power of love has its effects.

229.) Good morning, good afternoon, evening or goodnight is a blessing spoken from one to another. Some folk don't want the blessing.

230.) The feeling of wanting someone in a relationship and needing someone in one, determines the reason to walk away or stay.

231.) If all the energy we wasted on others was given back to us, we would be volts.

232.) Mistakes repeatedly made are no longer mistakes, it's purposely. Don't mistakenly choose wrong.

233.) Through thoughts and words, one has created his environment. Through thoughts and words one can change his environment.

234.) Today is not just another day. Today is just the beginning of what will become.

235.) My greatest strength is helping others. My weakness is helping others. I must learn to help myself and accept help from others.

236.) The worse reality is to accept that one has wasted years on someone not worth a minute of one's time.

237.) If you love someone, setting them free is not an option unless you yourself needs to be freed.

238.) Many negative thoughts can lead to a mental <u>breakdown</u>. Many positive thoughts can lead to a mental <u>breakthrough</u>. It depends on what you're thinking.

239.) Every brave person has encountered a fearful situation. How else would they become brave?

240.) Time is consistent, it is humans that change.

241.) Speak in a way that everyone that's hearing you, hears you.

242.) The way I am is the way I choose to be. I'm just as, I AM!

243.) A guilty conscience destroys the body and mind worse than diseases. Only the soul can heal a guilty conscience.

244.) Trust me when I say, "I love you" and trust me when I say, "I love you too." Trust me when I don't say I love you at all. Trust love and trust me.

245.) Talking is communication physically and tears are communication through the soul. My soul speaks often for the ones I love.

246.) If they've served their purpose in your life. Stop purposely trying to find reasons for them to stay.

247.) Pray in secret with all your heart and Praise out loud with all your heart and soul. Prayer changes you.

248.) People work hard to maintain the things they care about in life. Married people are an example of such.

249.) Keep it plain and simple when conversing with others. Sometimes the most intelligent people fail at communicating.

250.) Following direction doesn't guarantee you won't get lost.

251.) Remember to remember those who are important to you.

252.) Giving your all to the one you're loving is too much to give. You'll become a stranger to yourself.

253.) Suicide is an individual choice to end one's own life while affecting the lives of others.

254.) Everyone has been depressed about something or another. Most are depressed because of another.

255.) It cost nothing to show appreciation when someone does something nice for you. It could cost you a lot if you take someone for granted and they realize it.

256.) Procrastination delays success. Determination brings forth success. Be determined.

257.) If fear is considered weak, then how is it that fear control so many lives?

258.) A wealthy person doesn't need credit scores because wealth lasts a lifetime. A rich person if not careful can become poor if he has no credit or poor credit.

259.) Childhood experiences affect the choices and behavior of many in adulthood. Our world issues consist of adults with memories of both good and bad childhood experiences.

260.) A woman wants or need a strong man. Every man is strong in some type of way. Some men are mentally strong, some physically strong, and some spiritually strong. There's no such thing as a weak man.

261.) I and am, are separate words put together to describe oneness.

262.) Imagine if we could heal our bodies with our thoughts. Now, imagine if our thoughts were healed. Reality happens through thoughts.

263.) Understand that forgiveness is an act of communication with or without words that requires compassion in times of frustration.

264.) Being too busy trying to prove you are worth loving could be the mindset of a person who lacks selflove.

265.) Sacrifice doesn't always guarantee appreciation especially from one who is ungrateful.

266.) There's nothing more amazing than I AM. I AM created purposely.

267.) Property is a material thing that can be own. No person should ever be considered property if treated properly.

268.) "Whole life ahead of you" could be the very next second. Enjoy the present.

269.) Don't miss out on being loved by holding on to being rejected.

270.) Some have partners on the dance floor and still dance alone. Some have partners in relationships and are still being alone. It's best to just be alone than with a partner that doesn't move you.

271.) When the love is strong enough to survive anger, the Love is strong enough to survive anything.

272.) Not enough people participated in life's reunion because the universe didn't receive an invitation. We all need one another to survive.

273.) Love is an everyday celebration. Celebrate yourself!

274.) Never remember what you want to forget.

275.) I don't want to be better than anyone else. I want to be better than I have always been to myself.

276.) Lack of sleep and rest causes confusion of the mind. The world is full of sleepy people.

277.) We've been taught to prepare for rainy days. Umbrellas are needed on sunny days too.

278.) Funny how friends never know everything about friends but the enemies around them does.

279.) Communication is not just conversation. Sometimes communication is going days without speaking to one another.

280.) Being loyal to others and not trusting yourself is contradicting behavior.

281.) Take deep breaths to lower stress. Take deep breaths to raise vibration. Taking breaths is for living the next moment.

282.) Pain is a pleasure to feel when felt where numbness once existed.

283.) Money never change a person. It brings out the true person within.

284.) Do good deeds without expectations of payback later. Payback comes at an unexpected time.

285.) Thoughts come and go. Thoughts stay the same. Thoughts uncontrollable can cause a lot of pain.

286.) A cheater cheats himself every time he cheats.

287.) Miracles happen when miracles are expected not when least expected.

288.) Overthinking is far worse than putting no thought into a situation at all.

289.) Walk away when you are tired of running around in circles.

290.) If death is a part of life, then would you believe everyone lives forever.

291.) Human beings programed technology to help make life simpler, yet humans are destroying life instead.

292.) Just thinking of many ideas, requires just thinking.

293.) If I rise to the level of an angry man, I fall to the level of his feet because he stepped on my ego.

294.) A good day doesn't end just because trouble happens. It could become a better day if trouble is overcome.

295.) Racism is one of the most contagious diseases in the world. Infected people somehow affect others causing the disease to spread or lie dormant while slowly destroying soul.

296.) Animal lovers are proof that relationships work even when one can express himself with words and the other cannot.

297.) Being moved by our imagination takes us to our reality.

298.) The day I was born was for purpose. This exact moment was meant to be. Life is Felt On purpose. I AM purpose.

299.) If I intentionally put energy into ignoring you, you have my undivided attention.

300.) Words may never break your bones, but they can surely break your spirit.

301.) Your mouth can cause you more trouble than your mind could ever imagine.

302.) I would not turn my back on a friend in need. I would tell him to turn his back on me so that I may stand behind him instead.

303.) Learn to know your enemy just as much as your enemy knows you. Your enemy just might be you.

304.) Karma has no manners. It shows up unexpectedly and takes it's time to deliver.

305.) Let your heart be free to love and let your love be freely given.

306.) Why must people prove love when it's obvious that love exists within?

307.) Your mind creates your reality. How is it that your life is not as you want it to be?

308.) Don't cry because someone chose to leave you. Cry because they have sacrificed and tormented their soul out of ignorance of not knowing your value to them.

309.) There's nothing more important than love and there's nothing more important than trust. Love is not a mistake, trust the process.

310.) If ever in need to talk things over, practice in the mirror. If it's difficult seeing yourself, then it's probably best not to repeat the statement.

311.) Being oneself is difficult when one has lost himself in the process of pretending to be someone else.

312.) I'm living in a time where people are wishing death on the living and life to the dead.

313.) Never fear the fearless. Always be selfless to the selfish.

314.) Courage and humbleness are traits everyone needs to have in order to enjoy the journey of life.

315.) Today is not the time to worry about tomorrow. Tomorrow isn't the time to worry about today. Live!

****
****

For my daughters Brittney and Briana:

I love you because of who you were before I birthed you. I love you both-past, present, and future...~Ma/Mommy

1. What was your favorite quote?

2. Did you have to really think about what some of quote(s) were in reference to?

3. Did at least one quote help you?

4. Do you know anyone who could use one or more quotes to cause them to think about their situation?

Write your own quote(s) and notes that could help someone else as well:

My favorite Quote:

207.) Oh, how one forgets to appreciate memories until the day one is unable to remember a simple thing.

I thought of this quote while working with individuals with Dementia and Alzheimer's. The experience caused me to reflect and appreciate the things I took for granted such as, putting on clothes, brushing my teeth, or even seeing familiar faces especially love ones. It is a humbling experience to witness people who once knew everything needed for survival or happiness to not remember that those things even exist at certain moments of interactions.

And Eye Quote

*Poem

Have you ever loved someone until your soul
seemed to have cried?

Have you ever felt so much pain from the
love kept inside?

Have you ever been in love and your Spirit
began to grieve?

Have you ever hoped the love you give you'll
one day soon receive?

Have you found that special someone that
proved that love is true?

Have you taken the time to notice them or
push them away from you?

Do you not believe in love? Do you not
believe in you?

Can you open your love to others as they
have open theirs to you?

I believe in love and I believe in you!

Loving yourself first is proof that love is true.

I AM love.

By: Linette Tyler